PAULINE CATO'S
Northumbrian Choice

89 tunes from the Northumbrian tradition

DAVE MALLINSON PUBLICATIONS 1997

A session at the Tap and Spile, Morpeth

PAULINE CATO'S
Northumbrian Choice

First produced and published in England 1997 by Dave Mallinson Publications
3 East View, Moorside, Cleckheaton, West Yorkshire, England BD19 6LD
Telephone 01274 876388, *facsimile* 01274 865208, *e-mail* mally@mally.com *web* http://www.mally.com

ISBN 1 899512 38 1

A catalogue in print record for this title is available from the British Library

Cover photographs and design by Bryan Ledgard
All interior photographs by Danny Cato unless otherwise stated
Data input by David J Taylor and Greg Mallinson
Typesetting, data manipulation, harmony and page design by David J Taylor
First printed in England 1997 by The Digital Page Printing Company Limited, telephone 0113 238 0815

All rights reserved

Text set in Rotis Serif; music engraved in Petrucci using *Finale;* pages laid out in *QuarkXPress*
All tunes traditional except where stated otherwise, arranged Pauline Cato 1993

PAULINE CATO'S
Northumbrian Choice

Foreword

I first met Pauline Cato one afternoon in 1990 in the Northumberland village of Rothbury. We were making a *Folk on 2* programme about the famous Rothbury Traditional Music Festival where she had just won the open award for Northumbrian piping. We took Pauline and her pipes to a quiet corner of a field away from all the excitement and recorded her playing a spectacular knuckle-cracker called *The Acrobat*. What impressed me then - and still impresses me now - is her knowledge of and enthusiasm for the traditional music of her native Northumbria. Since that first meeting I have watched Pauline develop both as a performer and as a teacher and the present interest in the pipes is due in no small part to her efforts.

The music which has been made for the Northumbrian pipes over the years is an important, but often neglected, part of our musical heritage. That would be reason enough for producing this book and the accompanying recordings. But far more important is that what Pauline has done here is to bring together some terrific tunes. I know she enjoys playing them and I hope you will take pleasure from playing them - or hearing them - too.

Jim Lloyd
Presenter & Producer
Folk on 2

Recordings

Recordings of all the tunes herein are available on cassettes or compact discs: *Minstrel's Fancy* (DMPMC9701 and DMPCD9701) and *Bonny at Morn* (DMPMC9702 and DMPCD9702) either from Pauline, the publishers or from any stockist of traditional music. They feature Andy Gregory on bouzouki, George Welch on guitar and David J Taylor on octave mandolin.

Naturally, it is recommended that anyone with an interest in traditional music and the Northumbrian pipes makes every effort to purchase these two essential recordings. Please note that the chords given in this book may not correspond with those played on the recordings.

Contents

Alternate titles are in *italics*

Ben Cato, 'pet of the pipers'

Introduction

THIS BOOK is intended as an introduction to Northumbrian music for any instrument. Many of the tunes are very old traditional tunes from the north-east of England. However, several have come from other traditions and have been adopted in Northumberland and are played in numerous sessions. Northumberland's music has always been influenced by that of Scotland—this is obviously due in no small part to its geographical location. It is often difficult to discover the real origin of a tune since traditional music is constantly evolving. I find it particularly interesting that a tune from one tradition can be absorbed into another whilst taking on some of the characteristics of the new tradition.

The tunes I have chosen reflect the variety of Northumbrian music—slow airs, hornpipes, jigs, reels, slip jigs, rants and songs. Most of the tunes are already popular in Northumberland but there are a few lesser known ones which I feel deserve a wider audience. There are often one or more changes in tempo or rhythm within a set of tunes. This is a feature of Northumbrian music and in particular has developed from the tradition of playing slow air/jig or hornpipe/reel sets in Northumbrian competitions. There are several festivals and gatherings throughout the year in Northumberland and competitions still form an important part of these.

It is also hoped that this book will increase interest in Northumbrian music and inspire musicians to explore some of the other publications and recordings listed in the bibliography and discography at the back of this book.

The Northumbrian Pipes

THE MAJORITY of Northumbrian pipes are today pitched in F (more or less!). However, I am playing a G set on the accompanying recordings to enable other musicians to play along. The set of pipes used has a 17 key chanter with 5 drones and a switch for changing the key of the drones. Most of the tunes can nonetheless be played on a simpler set.

The tunes have been played in a traditional style, that is with staccato fingering. This is one of the most important features of the Northumbrian pipes. Part of the skill of playing the Northumbrian pipes is the ability to add ornamentation where the piper feels it is appropriate, unlike the Highland pipe tradition, where the written grace notes must be strictly adhered to. It is generally accepted that under-gracing is preferable to over-gracing as the Northumbrian pipes should produce a sweet but staccato sound. A lot of the sweetness comes naturally from the instrument but can be enhanced by the tasteful use of vibrato.

Buying Northumbrian Pipes

Pauline Cato

AS WITH all instruments, buying a set of pipes can be a minefield if you are not already a player. If at all possible, buy direct from a pipemaker so that you can discuss your exact needs. You will probably have to wait a while since pipes are generally made to order, but at least you will get exactly what is right for you. The pipemaker may also have pipes available for hire whilst you are waiting for yours to arrive.

If you are unable to see a pipemaker or are considering buying a set second hand or from a music shop, try to take someone with you who already knows about the pipes and can demonstrate them. Failing that, take note of the following:

1 Beware of pipes in a shop or on a stall that are on display in the sun or near anything hot.

2 If the pipes are on display with the chanter upside-down, there is a chance that excess oil could have run into the reed, thus rendering it useless.

3 The leather parts of the instrument, that is the bag, the bellows and the pads, should be supple and not dry.

4 The bag and bellows should be airtight.

5 The chanter keys should open quite easily when pressed and the chanter should not be warped at all.

At this point, it starts to become very difficult to describe exactly what to look for, so if you are thinking of buying a set you could start by contacting the Northumbrian Pipers' Society via the Bagpipe Museum in Morpeth, Northumberland for an up-to-date list of pipemakers.

Musical background

ALTHOUGH I have been playing the piano since I was five, I first started to learn the Northumbrian pipes at the age of 13. I attended Ashington High School, where Derek Hobbs, the music teacher, was very keen on the pipes. He arranged for Richard Butler, Piper to the Duke of Northumberland, to give lessons to six pupils, my sister and I included.

For the first year we were taught the basics of piping using keyless chanters. As the group progressed we were introduced to music from the *Peacock Collection* and started playing tunes with variations. At no point did Richard ever say "this is a hard tune" so we just did as we were told and learned to play them! Obviously, Richard's playing had a great influence on me and I feel I owe much of my success to the five years of instruction I received from him.

After about a year, Richard encouraged us to meet other pipers. The first event I went to was a meeting of the Northumbrian Musical Heritage Society run by Lance Robson in Morpeth. I began to attend regularly and it was here that I met Adrian Schofield for the first time. Adrian and I were to prove an important influence on each other. He introduced me to the music of Billy Pigg: exciting, fast and full of arpeggios! Adrian and I decided to begin playing duets together.

By this time I was also attending the monthly meetings of the Northumbrian Pipers' Society at the Sallyport Tower in Newcastle. I was introduced to pipemaker and society chairman Colin Ross and with Richard's recommendation, ordered my first set of pipes from him. They were delivered on Christmas eve 1984, the hire pipes were returned and the months I had spent the previous summer picking strawberries seemed worthwhile!

I was also a regular visitor to the Alnwick Pipers' Society, where the piping was led by the much respected Joe Hutton. I was subsequently invited to play at the piping evenings run by Patricia Jennings at Wallington. I feel that every musician you play with has an influence on you and consider myself fortunate to have been made welcome in so many piping circles in Northumberland and beyond.

With my new pipes, I entered a new and important phase of my musical career: that of competitions. The competitions for Northumbrian pipes run from April to November each year and are an essential part of the tradition. I entered both solo competitions (working my way up from beginners through intermediate to open) and also duet competitions with Adrian. I used to play the seconds or harmonies and learned to listen very closely to other musicians. I realise now what an important skill this is.

Adrian was keen on meeting the older generation of musicians and we visited many people, including Tommy Breckons, Diana Blackett-Ord, George Hepple (fiddle) and Annie Snaith (piano). We started to have piping evenings at Annie's, as she had done many years ago with her brother John Armstrong and piper Billy Pigg. By this time, my mother had also taken up the pipes so the three Catos and Adrian became regular visitors to Annie's. We invited Colin Ross and other pipers to join us and the evenings are still going strong more than ten years later.

Adrian, Colin and I formed a band called *Border Spirit* releasing the tape *Hindley Steel* in 1989. We performed mainly in the north-east but ventured twice to the Lorient Festival in Brittany before going our separate ways.

I went to Sheffield University in 1987 but made regular trips back to the north-east to play. During the summer months I was lucky enough to have a job at the Bagpipe Museum in Morpeth, working with curator Anne Moore. I also started playing with a ceilidh band in Sheffield which was to prove helpful in allowing my sense of rhythm to develop. The other musicians in the band wanted to play tunes in keys such as A major and B♭ major. Since I didn't want to admit that it couldn't be done on the pipes, I bought a 17-key chanter and learnt them anyway!

In 1989/90 my course (French, German and Swedish) meant that I had to spend a year abroad. I had a wonderful year travelling around Europe and met numerous good musicians, particularly in Germany.

On returning, I was appointed piper to the Mayor of Gateshead and took part in a number of projects with Alistair Anderson including *The Shipley Set*, a Czech/Northumbrian suite and the opera *Cullercoates Tommy*.

In 1992 I released my first solo album *The Wansbeck Piper*. I was doing a lot of solo concerts, in fact more that I could cope with since I had just taken up a job teaching languages. After teaching for a year, I decided that music was what I really wanted to do and became a full-time musician in 1993. My second album *Changing Tides* featuring fiddler Tom McConville followed in 1994. Due to popular demand, Tom and I formed a full time duo and in 1996 released *By Land and Sea* with guitarist Chris Newman. The success of this led to major tours in the UK and abroad.

It never ceases to amaze and delight me how the music of such a relatively small area is so popular throughout the world. I think that the music of our region is very special and hope that this collection will help to introduce it to many more musicians.

Pauline Cato

The Lemonville Jig

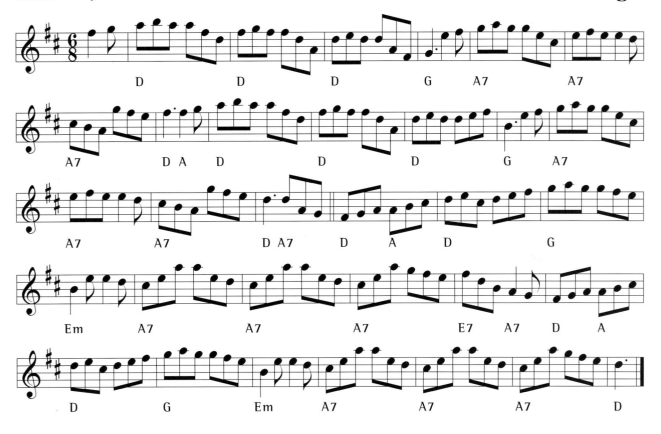

Harlequin's Jig

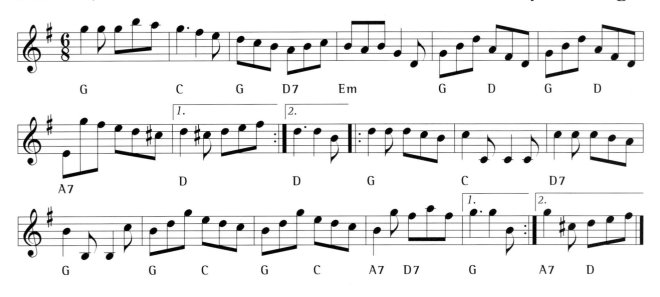

Pet of the Pipers

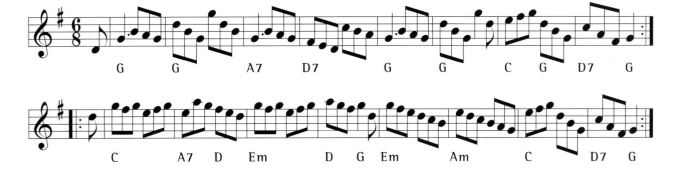

Saint Anne's Reel

Minstrel's Fancy, track 10, tune 1

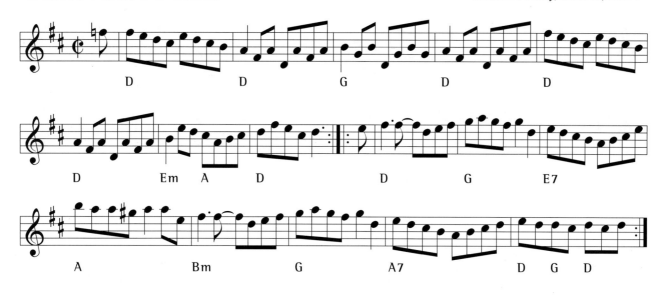

The three tunes on this page are 'adopted' tunes but are regularly played in Northumbrian music sessions.

Willafjord

Minstrel's Fancy, track 10, tune 2

The Mason's Apron

Minstrel's Fancy, track 10, tune 3

Minstrel's Fancy, track 11, tune 1

Rusty Gulley

Minstrel's Fancy, track 11, tune 2

Lads of Alnwick

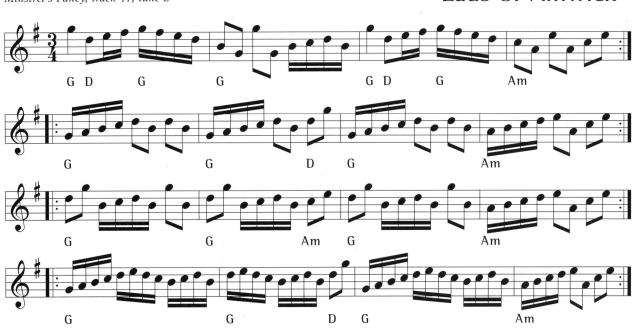

Alnwick Castle

Johnny Armstrong

Minstrel's Fancy, track 12

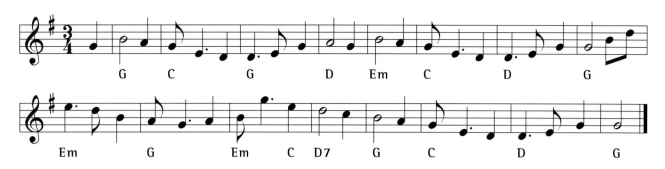

Keelman Ower the Land

Minstrel's Fancy, track 13, tune 1

The Redesdale Hornpipe was originally called *The Underhand* after a racehorse; it was written in Bb and was played back to front, i.e. the B music was first.

The Redesdale Hornpipe

Minstrel's Fancy, track 13, tune 2
Written by James Hill

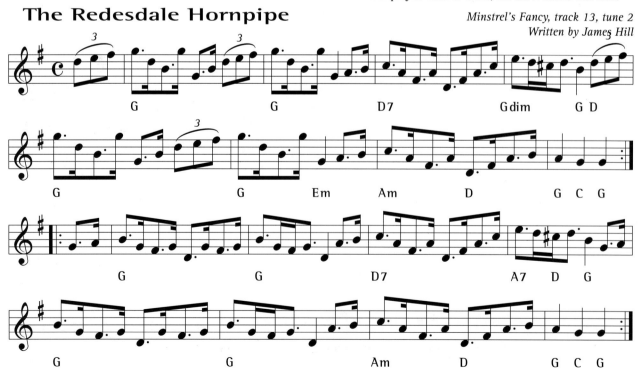

20

Minstrel's Fancy, track 14, tune 1

Derwentwater's Farewell

Minstrel's Fancy, track 14, tune 2
Written by T J Elliott

The Hesleyside Reel

Minstrel's Fancy, track 14, tune 3

Roxburgh Castle (G)

Minstrel's Fancy, track 14, tune 4

Roxburgh Castle (A)

Alston

Miss Thompson's Hornpipe

Minstrel's Fancy, track 15, tune 1

The Sheffield Hornpipe

Minstrel's Fancy, track 15, tune 2

22

Random

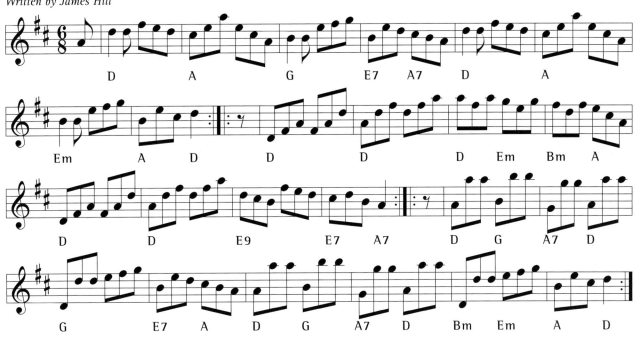

The Hawk

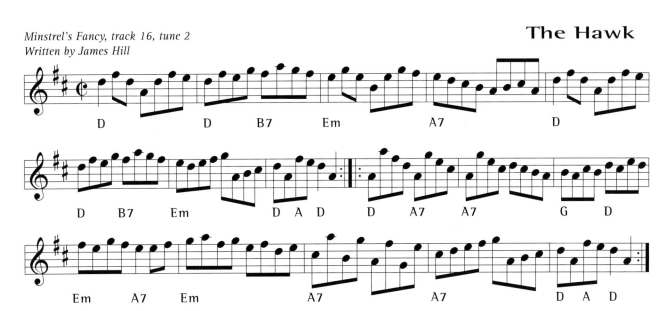

The De'il Amang the Tailors

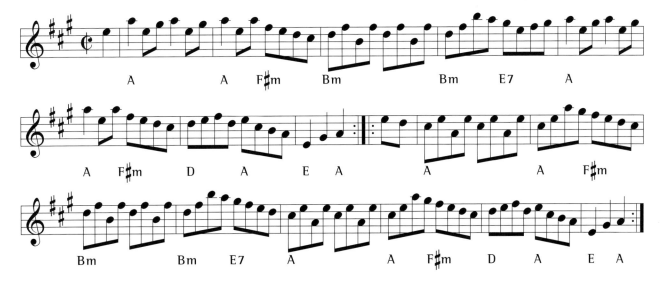

Lads of North Tyne

Minstrel's Fancy, track 17, tune 1

Minstrel's Fancy

Minstrel's Fancy, track 17, tune 2

24

Beadnell Harbour

Minstrel's Fancy, track 17, tune 3

Harvest Home

25

The Crooked Bawbee

Minstrel's Fancy, track 18, tune 1

The Friendly Visit

Minstrel's Fancy, track 18, tune 2

Annie Snaith's house, Elsdon

Annie Snaith's house has been the venue of numerous piping evenings, from the early days with Billy Pigg and her brother John Armstrong to the present day.

I'll Get Wedded in My Auld Claes
(The Hexham Quadrille)

The South Shore

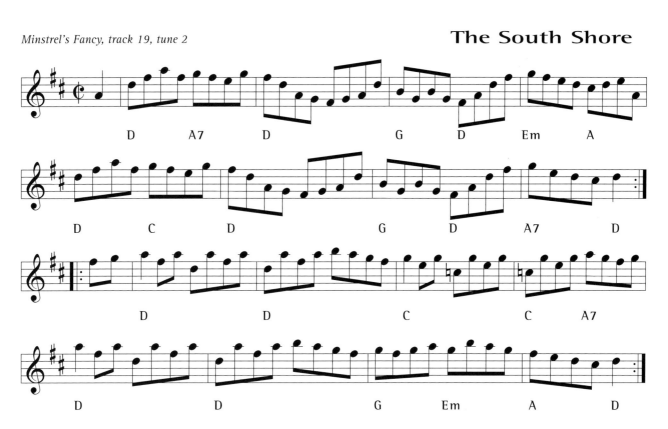

This tune has been attributed to James Hill.
However, it is also claimed that this was originally an
Irish tune called *The Scholar*.

Welcome to the Town Again

Bonny at Morn, track 1, tune 1

Holmes' Fancy

Bonny at Morn, track 1, tune 2

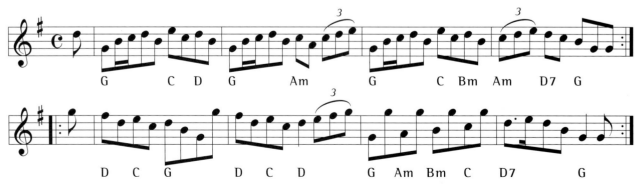

Small Coals and Little Money

Bob and Joan

Cuckold Come Out of the Amrey

The first five tunes on *Bonny at Morn* are amongst the oldest known Northumbrian tunes.

Liddell's is a good example of a hornpipe which can work well as a reel.

Liddell's

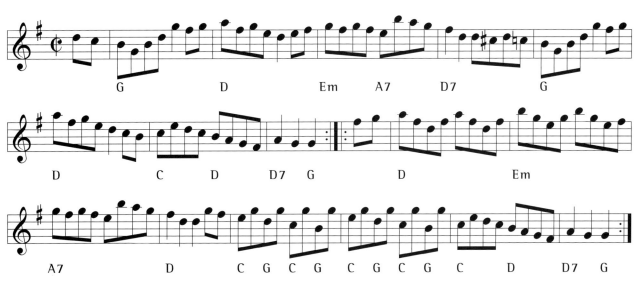

Whittingham Green Lane

Bonny at Morn, track 3, tune 1

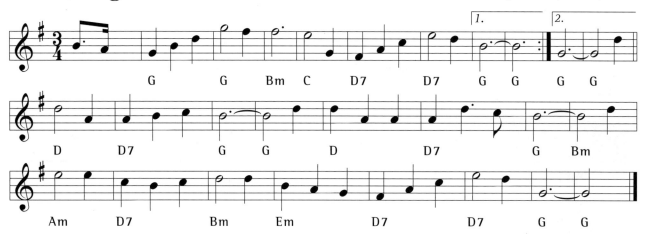

Come Ye Not from Newcastle?

Bonny at Morn, track 3, tune 2

St Nicholas' cathedral and the Black Gate, Newcastle

Canny Newcastle

Bonny at Morn, track 3, tune 3

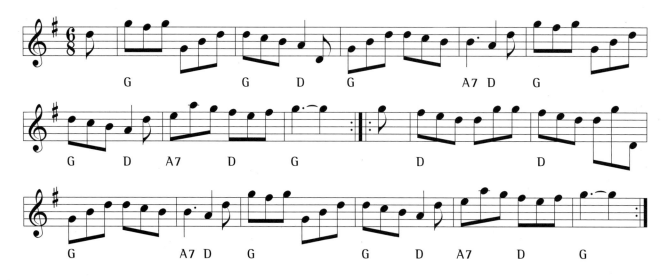

30

Bonny at Morn, track 4, tune 1
Written by Thomas Todd

The Barrington Hornpipe

Thomas Todd, a well-known piper from Choppington Station, circa 1889. Photograph used with permission, Cocks Collection, Morpeth Chantry Bagpipe Museum

Bonny at Morn, track 4, tune 2
Written by Robert Whinham

Remember Me

Hexham Races

Bonny at Morn, track 5, tune 1

Athole Highlanders (G)

Bonny at Morn, track 5, tune 2

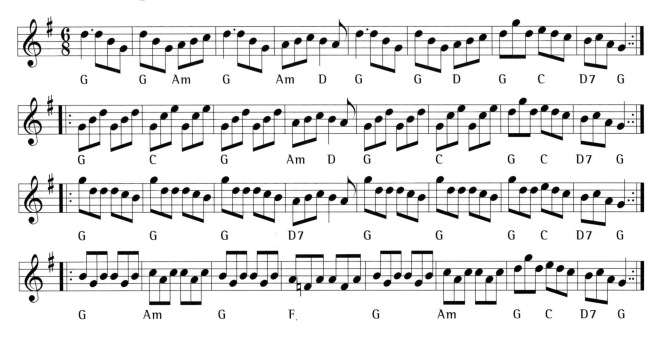

Athole Highlanders (A)

Bonny at Morn, track 5, tune 3

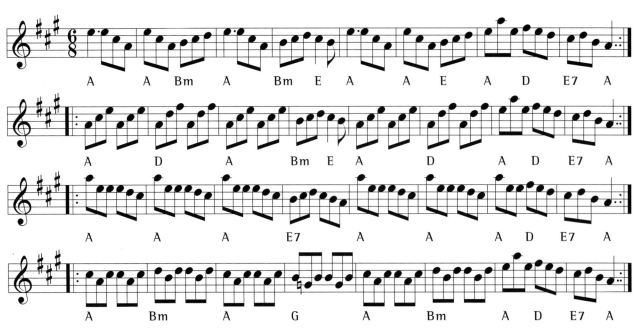

32

Bonny at Morn, track 6

Bonny at Morn

Bonny at Morn is a well-known Northumbrian song; this also works well as a slow air.

Bonny at Morn, track 7, tune 1

'Til the Tide Comes In

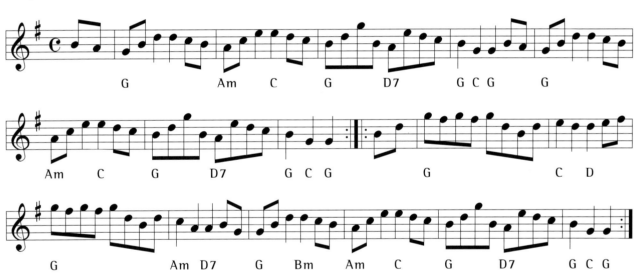

Bonny at Morn, track 7, tune 2

The Black Cock of Whickham

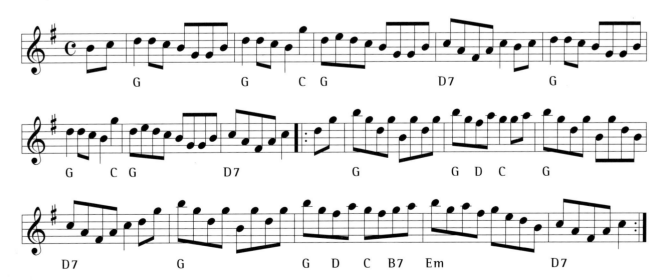

© *Dave Mallinson Publications 1997*

Durham Rangers

Bonny at Morn, track 8, tune 1

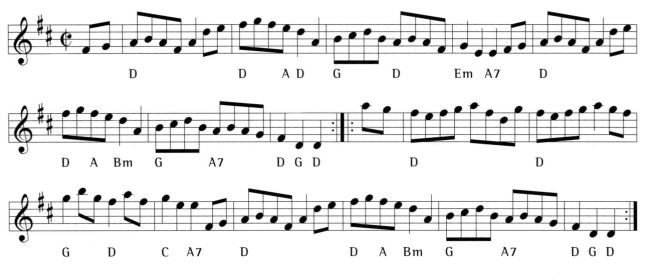

The Grand Chain

Bonny at Morn, track 8, tune 2

The Grand Chain is also known as *La Grande Chaîne*
and is believed to be of French-Canadian origin.

Morpeth Rant

Bonny at Morn, track 8, tune 3

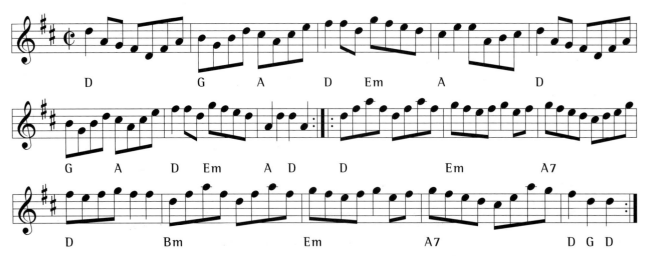

Bonny at Morn, track 9, tune 1

Ward's Brae

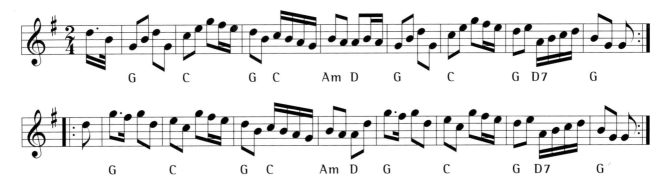

G   C   G   C   Am D   G   C   G   D7   G

G   C   G   C   Am D   G   C   G   D7   G

Bonny at Morn, track 9, tune 2

Winster Gallop

G   G   D7   G   Bm C   G   Am   D   G

G   G   G   Am D   D   D   D   D   G

Shown on this page is a standard set of simpler tunes for beginners.

Bonny at Morn, track 9, tune 3

Salmon Tails

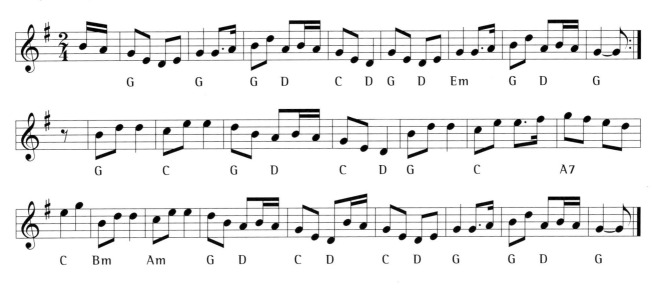

G   G   G   D   C   D G   D   Em   G   D   G

G   C   G   D   C   D G   C   A7

C   Bm   Am   G   D   C   D   C   D   G   G   D   G

Bonny at Morn, track 9, tune 4

Lamshaw's Fancy

G   G   Am   Am D7 G   G   G   D7   G

G   G   Am   Am   G   G   C   D7   G

© *Dave Mallinson Publications 1997*

The High Level Hornpipe

Bonny at Morn, track 10, tune 1
Written by James Hill; variation by Richard Butler

Variation on 1st part

The High Level Hornpipe and The New High Level were written in honour of the famous bridge over the Tyne and from which the celebrated band *The High Level Ranters* also took their name.

The High Level Bridge and the Swing Bridge over the River Tyne

The New High Level

Bonny at Morn, track 10, tune 2
Attributed to Robert Whinham

The old Barrasford ferry, north Tyne, circa 1950

Spootiskerry

Bonny at Morn, track 10, tune 3
Written by Ian Burns

A Wife of My Own

Bonny at Morn, track 11, tune 1

A Mile to Ride

Bonny at Morn, track 11, tune 2

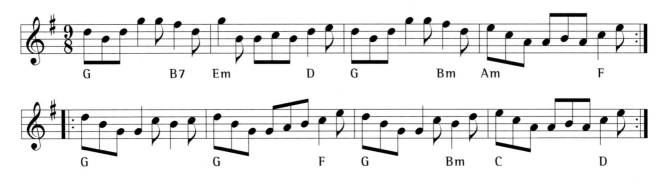

My Dearie Sits Ower Late Up

Bonny at Morn, track 11, tune 3

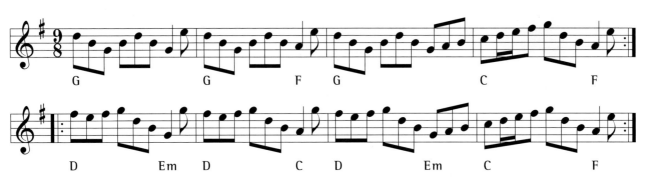

The Peacock Follows the Hen

Bonny at Morn, track 11, tune 4

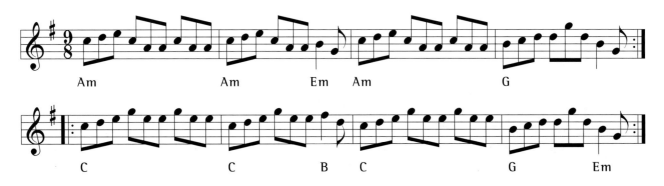

Woodhorn colliery

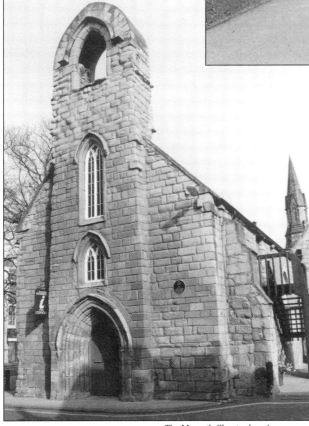

The Morpeth Chantry bagpipe museum

Two of Northumberland's major museums—the Woodhorn Colliery Museum near Ashington and the Morpeth Chantry, which houses the world-famous bagpipe museum.

Nae Good Luck Aboot the Hoose

Bonny at Morn, track 12, tune 1

40

Hareshaw Linn, near Bellingham

Bonny at Morn, track 12, tune 2

The Keel Row

Bonny at Morn, track 12, tune 3

Keep Your Feet Still Geordie Hinny

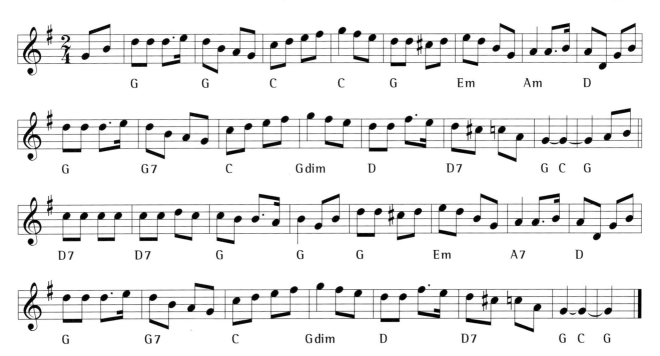

41

Proudlock's Hornpipe

Bonny at Morn, track 13, tune 1

Wade Hampton's Hornpipe

Bonny at Morn, track 13, tune 2
Written by Frank Livingston

Bellingham Boat

Bonny at Morn, track 14, tune 1

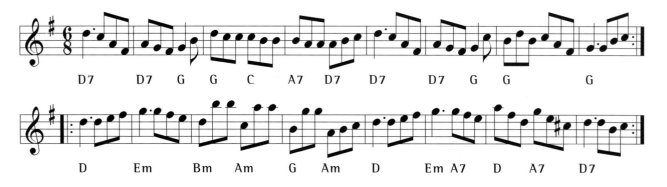

42

Bonny at Morn, track 14, tune 2

Lamb Skinnet

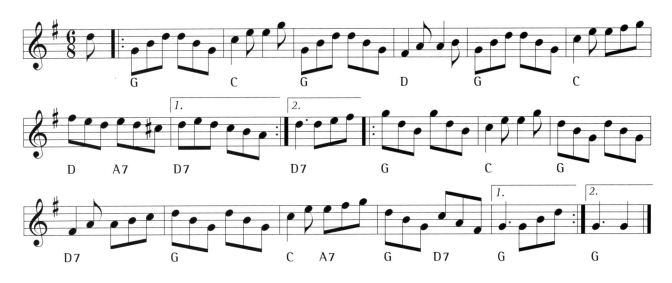

Bellingham Boat (below left) dates back to the days before the bridge was built and the boat was the only means of crossing the river.

Bonny at Morn, track 14, tune 3

Biddy the Bowl Wife

Bonny at Morn, track 14, tune 4

Saddle the Pony

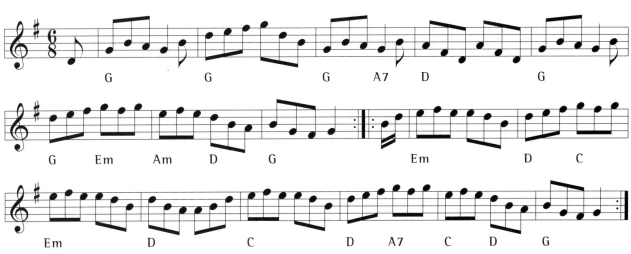

43

The Breamish

Bonny at Morn, track 15, tune 1

D   D   G Em   A   A7   D   D   D   D   G

Em A A   D D7   G   Em   D   D   Em   A7

G   D   G   Em   D   D B7 E7   A7   G D

Linhope Loup

Bonny at Morn, track 15, tune 2

D A7 D   Em   D   D A7

D   Em   A7   D   D   G Em

A   G A7   D   G Em A7   D

The Breamish is a beautiful river in north Northumberland. The waterfall Linhope Spout is in the Breamish valley. To 'loup' means to jump.

Opposite are four tunes very popular with Northumbrian pipers.

Linhope Spout

44

Jimmy Allen

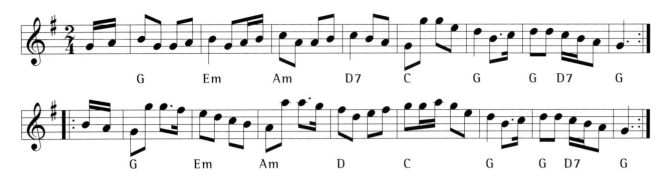

Because He was a Bonny Lad

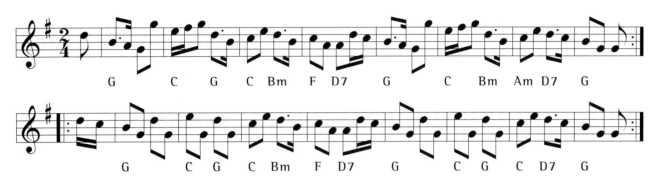

Buttered Peas

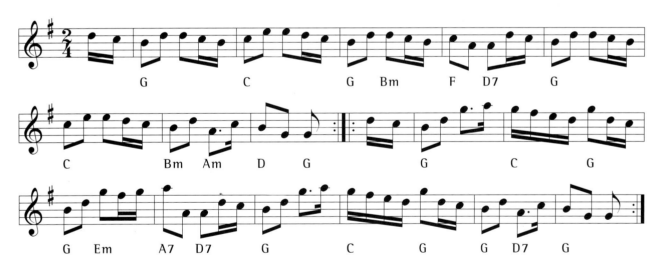

Herd on the Hill

Millicent's Favourite

Bonny at Morn, track 17, tune 1

Millicent, the fell pony circa 1960

Madame Bonaparte

Bibliography

The Coquetdale Garland — Archie Dagg

Published by The Northumbrian Pipers' Society:

Northumbrian Pipers' Tunebook	ISBN 902510 00 2
Northumbrian Pipers' Second Tunebook	ISBN 0 902510 08 8
Northumbrian Pipers' Third Tunebook	ISBN 0 902510 11 8
Northumbrian Pipers' Duet Book	ISBN 0 902510 09 6
The Charlton Memorial Tunebook	ISBN 0 902510 03 7
Peacock's Tunes	ISBN 0 902510 07 X

Published by Graham Dixon (Random Publications):

The Lads Like Beer (The Fiddle Music of James Hill)	ISBN 0 9511572 0 5

Published by Graham Dixon (Wallace Music):

Remember Me (The Fiddle Music of Robert Whinham)	ISBN 0 9511572 1 3

Published by Rossleigh Music:

The Piper's Companion Book 1	Derek Hobbs
The Piper's Companion Book 2	Derek Hobbs
The Piper's Companion Book 3	Derek Hobbs
The Piper's Companion Book 4	Derek Hobbs
Bewick's Footsteps	Derek Hobbs
The Jack Armstrong Tune Book	Jack Armstrong

Published by Dragonfly Music:

The Northumbrian Piper's Yellow Pocket Book	Matt Seattle	ISBN 1 872277 14 4
The Northumbrian Piper's Green Pocket Book	Matt Seattle	ISBN 1 872277 15 2
The Morpeth Rant	Matt Seattle	ISBN 1 872277 01 2

Discography

Pauline Cato:

Pauline Cato	*The Wansbeck Piper*	PC01 1992 CD or cassette
Pauline Cato with Tom McConville	*Changing Tides*	PC02 1994 CD or cassette
Pauline Cato and Tom McConville with Chris Newman	*By Land and Sea*	TC01 1996 CD or cassette
Pauline Cato and others	*Minstrel's Fancy*	DMP9701 CD or cassette
Pauline Cato and others	*Bonny at Morn*	DMP9702 CD or cassette

Other Northumbrian releases featuring the pipes:

Alistair Anderson	*Steel Skies*	Own label Cassette only
Border Minstrels	*Echoes from the Hills*	BM001 Cassette only
Border Minstrels	*From Hills to Shore*	BM002 Cassette only
Richard Butler	*Reflections*	NR001 Cassette only
The High Level Ranters	*Gateshead Revisited*	CGRC005 Cassette only
Joe Hutton with Hannah Hutton	*The Border Piper*	CGRL006 Cassette only
Joe Hutton	*Northumbrian Piper*	CD or cassette
Billy Pigg	*Legendary Recordings*	BK017 Cassette only
Syncopace	*Syncopace*	CROW226 CD or cassette
Kathryn Tickell	*On Kielderside*	SDL343 CD or cassette
Kathryn Tickell	*Borderlands*	CROW227 CD or cassette
Kathryn Tickell	*Common Ground*	CROW210 CD or cassette
The Kathryn Tickell Band	*The Kathryn Tickell Band*	CROW220 CD or cassette
The Kathryn Tickell Band	*Signs*	CROW230 CD or cassette

Many of the recordings and publications shown on this page are widely available at the time of going to print; in case of difficulty locating them, please contact the publishers